MAISIE TAYLOR

WOOD IN ARCHAEOLOGY

D1429988

SHIRE ARCHAEOLOGY

TITLES IN THE SHIRE ARCHAEOLOGY SERIES
with their series numbers

Cover illustration
Pinewood figure of iron-age date from Roos Carr, Humberside.
The eyes were inlaid with quartzite pebbles.
(Kingston upon Hull City Museums)

Published by
SHIRE PUBLICATIONS LTD
Cromwell House, Church Street, Princes Risborough,
Aylesbury, Bucks, HP17 9AJ, UK.

Series Editor: James Dyer

ISBN 0 85263 537 0

First published 1981

Printed in Great Britain by
C.I. Thomas & Sons (Haverfordwest) Ltd,
Press Buildings, Merlins Bridge, Haverfordwest.

Contents

List of illustrations

Preface

Wood has always played an important part in the life of man, and trees have provided food, fuel and other raw materials from the earliest times. The study of archaeological wood has long been neglected. This is partly because the survival of wood over a long period of time is rare and only occurs where the circumstances of the burial are exceptional. Another problem arises when wood which has been preserved under exceptional circumstances is dug up. As soon as this wood is disturbed, then the circumstances which led to its survival are also disturbed and the wood will start to decay and collapse very rapidly.

This book attempts to introduce the subject of archaeological wood to the reader who is a specialist neither in archaeology nor in botany. Information about the subject is available but it is widely scattered and this may make it difficult for the non-specialist to find relevant works. An obvious source of information on some of the latest and most important work on archaeological wood is to be found in the *Somerset Levels Papers*. These small books are published annually and cover each new season's work in the peat landscape of the Somerset Levels.

Carole Keepax taught me the rudiments of wood identification at the Ancient Monuments Laboratory in London, and I am extremely grateful to her for 'starting me off' in the subject. A number of people have helped in the preparation of the manuscript of this book, mainly by reading and commenting upon it; amongst them I should especially mention Frank Green of Southampton University and Martin Jones of Oxford. Veryan Heal of Cambridge and Dr John Peter Wild of Manchester also read the manuscript at an early stage. John Shepherd of the Institute of Archaeology in London and my brother, Nigel, of the Surrey County Library Service both pursued and supplied a number of obscure references. Francis Pryor encouraged this work from the beginning and has provided much practical help as well as ideas.

Special help with illustrations was provided by Mary Cra'ster of the University Museum of Archaeology and Ethnology in Cambridge, Glynis Edwards of the Ancient Monuments Laboratory in London and Dr J. M. Coles of the Somerset Levels Project and Cambridge University.

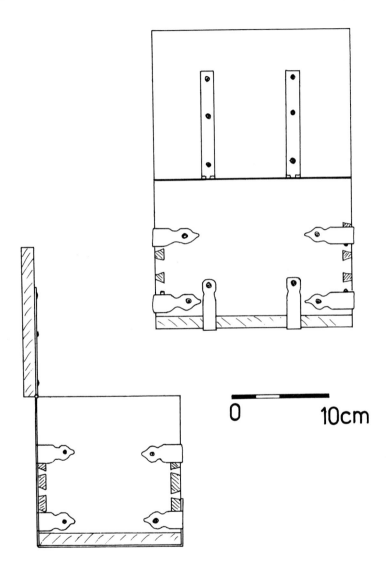

Fig. 1. This reconstruction of a Roman chest from Bradwell Villa was only possible through the careful examination of the corrosion products on the iron straps. It was possible to make out the dovetail joints and the method of construction through microscopic study of the wood replaced by iron salts.

1
Burial conditions and the preservation of wood

The remains of wood may be preserved in archaeological deposits by one of six means:

(a) By conditions of extreme waterlogging

Permanent waterlogging preserves organic material by excluding air, thus creating anaerobic conditions, so that organisms that would normally destroy the wood are unable to survive. This condition may be widespread in peat bogs but conditions of waterlogging can occur unexpectedly on sites, usually in ponds or wells. When oak becomes waterlogged, or if the ground water is acid, the wood may be helped in its preservation by tannin in the wood and water.

(b) By conditions of extreme desiccation

Excavators in Europe are unlikely to find wood preserved by conditions of extreme aridity but wood in standing buildings is often very hard and dry. Extreme dry conditions lead to the preservation of wood (and other organic materials) because the organisms that destroy wood under normal conditions cannot survive without moisture.

(c) By carbonisation

Carbonised wood or charcoal does not deteriorate in the ground because it is chemically stable and very few organisms can digest carbon. Charcoal occurs in varying quantities on virtually every site in the world. The condition of the charcoal in archaeological deposits is largely governed by the completeness of the original carbonisation process.

(d) By association or replacement by metal corrosion products or minerals

Wood that has been replaced by metal corrosion products probably occurs much more frequently than is reported. Wood remains preserved in this way are not always easy for the untrained eye to detect and they are probably often destroyed by over-enthusiastic cleaning (fig. 1). Any metal object may have wood preserved with it but it is more likely to occur in sockets or at the hafting points of tools and weapons. Often the wooden handles are preserved and may be quite visible to the naked eye. The corrosion products associated with any metal object should be examined closely for organic remains. Where the object does appear to have associated organic material, these remains may be only a shadow which will not survive attempts at removal or energetic cleaning. The replacement of wood by mineral salts may occur on sites on chalk or limestone and this has allowed the timber lacing of hillforts to be examined in some detail. Replaced wood often varies in condition: it may sometimes be soft enough to break and identify as if it were charcoal but at other times more sophisticated methods may be needed. If the wood remains only as a cast of its original structure it may need to be examined under an electron scanning microscope before it can be identified.

(e) As an impression in baked clay

Organic material, such as grain, grass or wood, which becomes incorporated into clay before it is fired may be burnt out, leaving an impression in the clay after firing. If this impression is sharp enough, it may be possible to identify the species.

(f) As a stain

Occasionally the wood may rot away entirely but the former presence may be indicated by a stain remaining in the ground (fig. 2).

Fig. 2. These Roman waterpipes from Colchester were made of wood. None of the wood survived but it was possible to deduce the presence of the pipes because of the iron clamps which originally held the pipe sections together and because of the stains left in the soil by the decayed wood. Only meticulous excavation techniques can prevent this kind of evidence from being destroyed. (Photograph: P. Crummy, Colchester Archaeological Trust.)

2
The exploitation of woody plants in the past

The possibilities for the exploitation of woody plants in antiquity are vast and we can be sure that man exploited the plant material around him from earliest times. Wood from many trees occurs regularly on sites but twigs and branches that have ended up as firewood do not represent the total possible exploitation of that species. The appearance of a species on a site in one form suggests that it was available for exploitation in other forms. Wood may have been brought to a site for the preparation of dyes from its bark, for instance. Trees in the immediate locality of a site, and occasionally more distant, would have provided fuel, food and drugs as well as a number of other valuable commodities. It seems likely that different species were often selected for their different characteristics and properties, with the remains of virtually everything ending up in the hearth sooner or later. Trees with special properties or that provided important raw materials were probably sought over long distances.

There is also growing evidence that wood management may have been practised from at least the neolithic period. Coppicing and pollarding ensured a constant supply of wood and timber and other raw materials within a small radius of a settlement (fig. 3), whereas simple clearance of the woods would have meant that items such as stakes, withies and osiers for basketry and so on would have gradually become more difficult to find as they do not occur naturally in the forest. Wood management was practised widely until recently (fig. 4) and does not require the destruction of the vegetation but guarantees a reliable supply of wood. Forestry, whereby the harvesting of the trees also means their destruction, seems to be a modern concept.

Vast amounts of wood must have been used at all periods in history and prehistory so that any site that produces wood can only provide a small glimpse of the full picture. Archaeological finds such as carpentry tools may suggest how sophisticated the woodworker had become (fig. 5) and occasionally finds may be made that will illustrate the techniques that were possible (fig. 6). Wood can also be used and reworked any number of times. Each reworking would provide waste material that would have probably found its way into the hearth. Finally, the object itself, having outlived its useful life, would also have found its way on to the fire, or possibly the rubbish heaps. With this in mind, it is important to consider the factors that lead to the deposition of the wood. Except on sites which were suddenly and totally inundated or in waterlogged features incorporating wood in their construction (for example well linings) wood is not usually

coppicing

pollarding

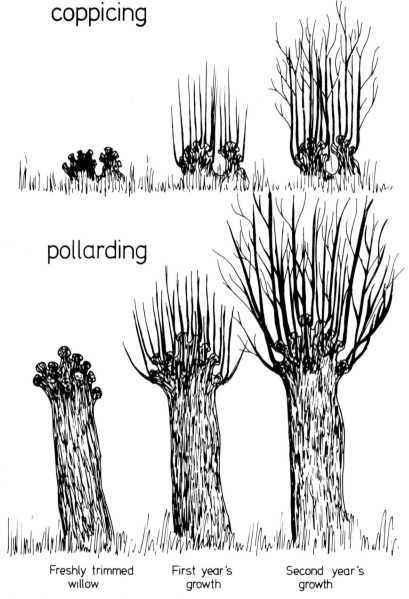

| Freshly trimmed willow | First year's growth | Second year's growth |

Fig. 3. Coppicing and pollarding used to be common activities, especially in managed woodland. The trees are cut back every few years for the poles that they produce. The length of time between the cutting of the poles depends on what they are required for.

Fig. 4. These modern pollards of willow are often found in the Fens of eastern England. The tree on the extreme left was pollarded exactly one year before the next two trees in the row, which are newly trimmed. (Photograph: M. Taylor.)

preserved *in situ,* an important factor in the interpretation of archaeological remains.

Plant remains, including wood, are often used as a basis for interpreting the ancient landscape. There are a number of problems in this kind of work because there are so many factors affecting the ways that the plants arrived on the sites where they are found. They may have arrived by accident, been brought there by man or simply been growing in the vicinity. Archaeological wood is usually found in the form of odd pieces of twigs or branches or the remains of artefacts. Where a piece of wood has been used for a specific purpose, such as a handle, it is not unreasonable to assume that the wood was chosen for particular characteristics and qualities. Charcoal can occur on a site from a great variety of sources. Local vegetation may have been burnt off, by accident or on purpose, by man and the charcoal found its way into pits, ditches and suchlike in the area. Wood that has been burnt intentionally as firewood may have been chosen for a particular purpose, such as firing a kiln or oven. Generally, however, it seems fairly safe to assume that waste from woodworking, together with all sorts of other bits and pieces, would have eventually been put on the fire.

Through a greater understanding of the possibilities and properties of the different species of tree the archaeologist can be helped towards a more balanced and imaginative interpretation of the wood remains from his site. Trees can produce a large number of raw materials, other than wood, and all the woods display different characteristics that influence their strength and potential as fuel.

Fig. 5. Indirect evidence for wood and woodworking may come from the tools of the carpenter. These Roman carpenter's tools are remarkably modern in appearance and perhaps indicate the sophistication of the craft at the period. The mitre square comes from Canterbury and the plane from Verulamium. (Drawings: plane, S.S. Frere and the Society of Antiquaries; mitre square, after Tatton-Brown, courtesy of Canterbury Archaeological Trust.)

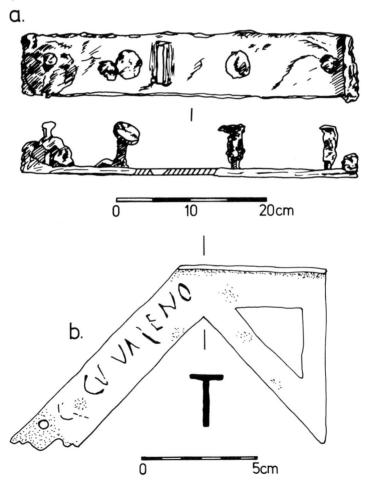

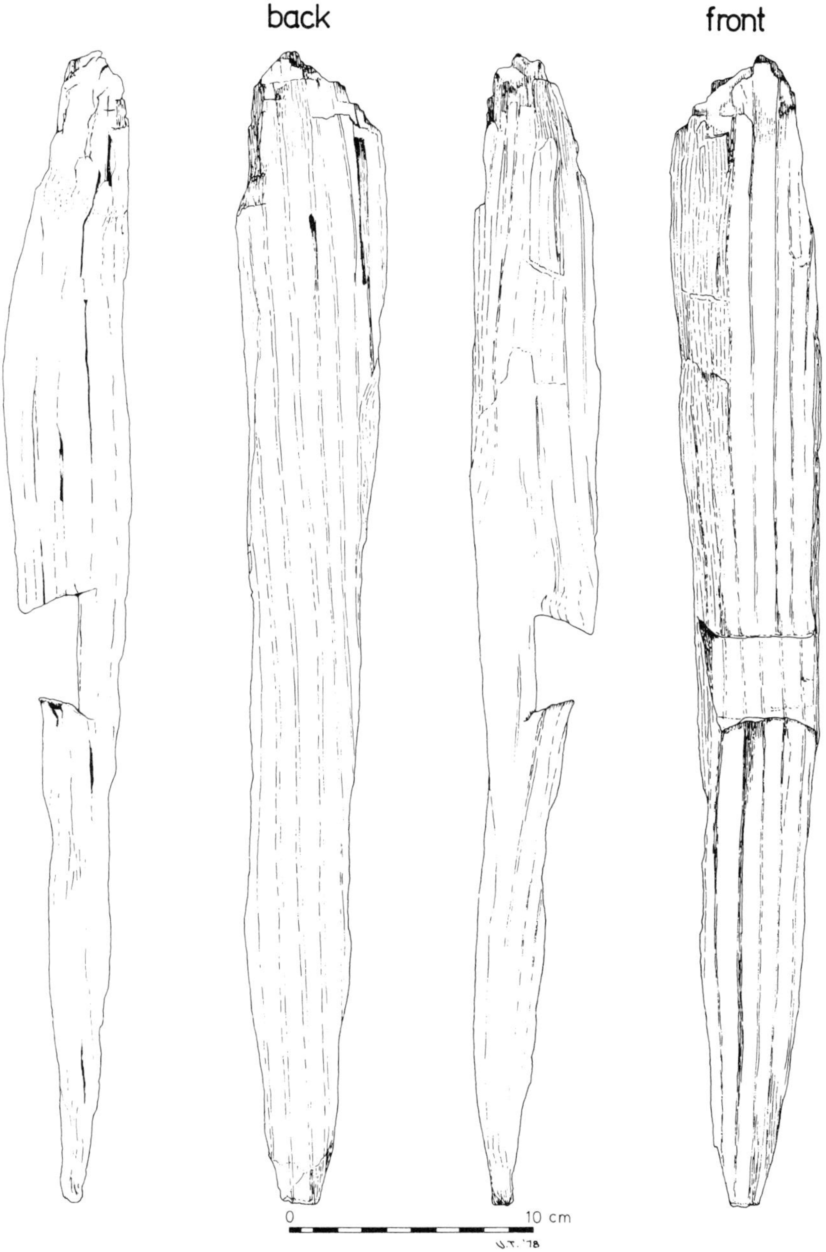

back   front

0   10 cm

Fig. 6. This piece of oak from Fengate was reused as a stake to hold back the side of a shallow well in the early iron age. Previously it had been carefully chiselled to form the neat dovetail joint. There are examples of sophisticated joinery from the bronze age onwards but this is probably the oldest dovetail yet found.

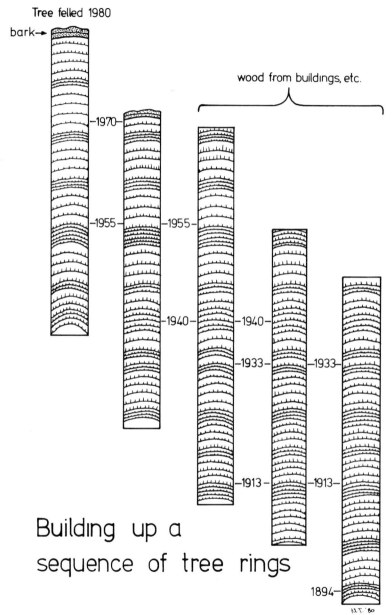

Fig. 7. This diagram shows how patterns in tree rings are recognised and matched with older and younger timber to build up a continuous sequence. This is a simplification because many examples from different trees are needed and sophisticated statistics are applied to these sequences before they are acceptable.

3
Carbon-14 and dendrochronology

The archaeologist may take samples of wood and charcoal from his site for different purposes. The commonest reason for sampling charcoal is to submit it to carbon-14 dating because a reliable date can be obtained from a small sample, as charcoal is almost pure carbon. It is important that the charcoal submitted for dating should be from a very secure archaeological context, since charcoal can easily be redeposited. The carbon-14 date tells us when the wood was carbonised, not when it was buried. As charcoal can lie on the surface of the ground for many years before finding its way into a pit or ditch, the best charcoal for dating comes from a hearth, where the spread of age of the wood on the fire can be assumed to be quite small, although timber of some considerable age (perhaps two hundred to three hundred years) could be present in logs from substantial trees. Taking samples for carbon-14 dating is a specialised process and it is usually best to consult the laboratory that will be dating the samples. However there are certain rules that remain constant. It is very important that the sample should remain completely uncontaminated. Wood or charcoal that is taken for carbon-14 dating should not come into contact with any fungicide, insecticide or conserving medium, such as the commonly used water-soluble wax polyethylene glycol. It is best to handle samples which are to be submitted for dating as little as possible. It is not even necessary to clean a sample to any great extent as it will have to be thoroughly purified in the laboratory before it is processed. A sample of waterlogged wood may be dried, either in a drying oven (not a cooking oven) or, protected, in the air if it is necessary. The wood may collapse and disintegrate but this is not important in the dating process. The sample should be packed in heavy duty polythene, not in the thin polythene bags that are used for wrapping food. Glass containers are not advisable because they are so fragile. Paper is totally unsuitable. The sample should be wrapped in one polythene bag and placed, with a label carrying full details of the sample, inside another. The label should not be inside the inner bag and the details of the sample should not be written on the outside of the bag because they are liable to be rubbed off. The quantities of wood and charcoal required for a date vary according to the quality of the sample submitted and the methods and preferences of the laboratory that processes the material. For charcoal between 8 and 12 grams should be submitted. The quantity depends on the quality of the original carbonisation process, which is not easy for the layman to judge. More wood is needed, although the exact quantity depends on the standard of preservation. Between 10 and 30 grams should be submitted.

Another form of dating for wood is dendrochronology or tree-ring dating. Probably everyone knows that the age of a tree can be worked out by counting its growth rings but a refinement of this technique may well tell the expert when the tree lived. The reason why trees lay down their growth rings in the way that they do is the different patterns of growth during the different seasons of the year. Most trees grow rapidly during the spring but this tails off until there is virtually no growth in winter. The conditions in which the trees grow affect the rate of growth and this will be reflected in the relative thickness and density of the growth rings. The weather and ground water are the two main factors which affect this growth, excessive water generally producing thicker rings whilst drought causes much thinner rings to be formed. The pattern created by these differences will be similar in all the trees of the same species growing in the same area. By comparing the patterns of recently felled trees and overlapping them with wood from trees of a much greater age, it is possible to build up a sequence of rings back through time (fig. 7). The most successful case where this was done was in America, where the bristlecone pine was found to be a very long-lived tree, many specimens living for four thousand years. Long dead trees lying about, preserved by the dry atmosphere in the area, were used to extend the sequence of tree rings back for hundreds and then thousands of years. Sections of these trees were then subjected to carbon-14 dating. As the wood was of known date it was possible to pinpoint anomalies in the dates obtained by the carbon-14 method and draw a graph in an attempt to calibrate the date curve and increase its accuracy. Similar work is being attempted in Britain. The main tree used is oak because it lays down strong rings. The dendrochronology of wood from medieval churches and houses now extends back into late Saxon times. Other work is going on with the bog-oaks from the Fens in eastern England. These trees represent the forests that died because of the rising water table in the area thousands of years ago. A record of tree rings and carbon-14 dates is being built up from these trees when they are dragged out of the peat for the drainage of farmland. This chronology will be a 'floating chronology' at first because it will not join up with the more modern tree ring sequences. The eventual aim would be to have a continuous record of tree rings dating far back into prehistory so that the wood can be compared and dated and used to date the objects that were buried in association. Some large sites, such as the Somerset Levels in the west of England, are able to establish their own floating chronology for a site. As research continues it may become possible for some of these floating chronologies to be joined up and securely dated.

The main laboratories specialising in radio-carbon dating are at the Atomic Research Establishment at Harwell, at Cambridge University, and the British Museum Research Laboratory in London. Radio-carbon dating is extremely expensive and generally would be outside the resources of amateur groups or individuals. A number of universities have research departments which would take samples from outside if they fitted in with that department's research programme. Most of these establishments will advise enquirers about the possibility of dating samples but generally, unless the date is required to solve a problem of more than local interest, the acquisition of carbon-14 dates is a most expensive process.

Fig. 8. *(Top)* The point of a bronze-age stake as recovered wet from the peat (broken as it passed through a peat-cutting machine). *(Bottom)* An early neolithic stake after conservation by Carbowax; the shrinkage is eight per cent but the facets and colour are preserved. *(Centre)* Two late neolithic stakes allowed to dry naturally, without conservation; they originally matched in size the upper wet and lower waxed pieces. Scale in centimetres. (Photograph: J. M. Coles.)

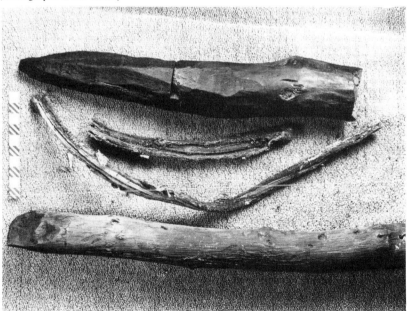

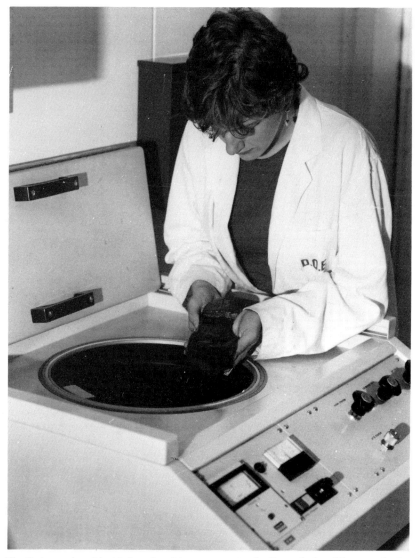

Fig. 9. A wooden object being placed in an apparatus for freeze-drying. (Photograph: Ancient Monuments Laboratory. Crown Copyright — reproduced with permission of the Controller of Her Majesty's Stationery Office.)

4
Conservation of wood

Conservation of wood is a long and skilled process which has only recently been developed. In earlier times people tried to dry out wood or preserve it in alum but these were not particularly successful methods. Wood which has been waterlogged is very difficult to dry out satisfactorily because it usually distorts and collapses rapidly when the drying process begins (fig. 8). This is because wood has two main components in its structure: lignin and cellulose. Many factors contribute to the decay of wood but the structure of archaeological wood is particularly affected by the loss of the cellulose because of the waterlogging. Cellulose is easily converted into sugars and then dissolved away. The spaces that are left in the structure of the wood are then filled with water, which acts as a cushion and buoys up the structure. When the wood is removed from its waterlogged conditions this water dries out and the structure begins to collapse. This process begins as soon as the wood is uncovered, but it can be slowed down if the wood is kept wet. It is important, if the wood is to be conserved to resemble its original form, to fill the spaces left by the cellulose with a suitable substance before they collapse, or to dry it under specially controlled conditions. The wood is dried nowadays by using very sophisticated freeze-drying equipment which only larger conservation laboratories would have (fig. 9). A more generally applied technique is to immerse the wet wood in a solution of polyethylene glycol (PEG), tradename 'Carbowax', at a solution of 25 per cent PEG to 75 per cent water (fig. 10). PEG is a water-soluble wax and when the wood is saturated with it the spaces in the wood structure are filled with the wax solution, taking the place of the water. When the saturation of the piece is complete it can be dried out and, except for slight shrinkage, with careful cleaning of the surface it should look very like it did originally. The process is very slow, perhaps taking up to nine months to process a large object, but in skilled hands the results can be very acceptable. The logistical problems of treating larger objects, such as boats, are obvious and large tanks and skilled conservators are needed where a wreck, for example, is to be dismantled, conserved and rebuilt — a very specialised branch of the study of archaeological wood.

When an archaeologist finds wood in a waterlogged condition on a site there are a number of things that can be done which do not require any specialised knowledge, only common sense. First the object should be photographed in the ground in case it does not survive being lifted. It should not be allowed to dry out but may be lightly sprayed with water and kept covered with polythene if it cannot be lifted immediately. If the weather is hot the wood should be protected

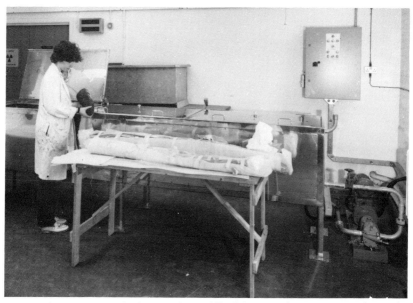

Fig. 10. Bronze-age wood about to be stabilised in a modern treatment plant using polyethylene glycol. (Photograph: Ancient Monuments Laboratory. Crown Copyright — reproduced with permission of the Controller of Her Majesty's Stationery Office.)

Fig. 11. The Rowlands track site in the Somerset Levels. The photograph was taken in late morning in June 1976, at the height of a drought. The site has been covered with a double layer of polythene sheeting, sealed along its edges to protect the peat and wood from drying out during the warmest part of the day. (Photograph: B. J. Orme.)

Fig. 12. Excavations of the Abbot's Way in the Somerset Levels. In the foreground wood is being cleaned with a paintbrush and water. In the middle distance wood is being watered with a sponge and bucket. The excavated part of the track is kept damp by the plastic sheeting in the background. Work is carried out from planks over the track or from toe-boards on the peat surface. (Photograph: J. M. Coles.)

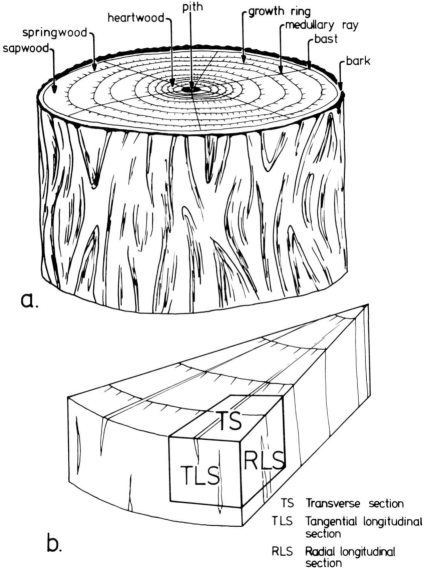

Fig. 13. *(Top)* The general structure of a branch or log of softwood. *(Bottom)* This wedge of wood, taken from a log, shows the three faces required for examination if an identification is to be made. Some woods, such as oak, are very distinctive and can easily be identified by eye, or with a hand lens; others need microscopic examination.

through the main heat of the day and from the direct rays of the sun (fig. 11). The wood can be excavated during either the morning or the evening, when it is cooler. Extremes of cold are equally damaging, causing cracking. Wood which has been waterlogged should be lifted carefully and supported at all times even though it may look robust. The techniques for excavating waterlogged wood on a large scale are very specialised and are seen at their best in the pioneering work done by the Somerset Levels Project (fig. 12). Ancient waterlogged wood is usually much more brittle than modern wood and may fall apart under its own weight. Once lifted, the wood should be kept wet and supported and should be drawn and recorded quickly, especially if it was not possible to do this thoroughly while it was still in the ground. It may prove impractical to conserve a piece or it may simply confound all attempts at conservation and fall apart within a few hours. Generally wood can be preserved for some time by simply keeping it wet and well supported. The best and most accessible advice about conserving wood is found in a series of monographs published by the National Maritime Museum in London and in a book called *Conservation in the Field* by Elizabeth Dowman.

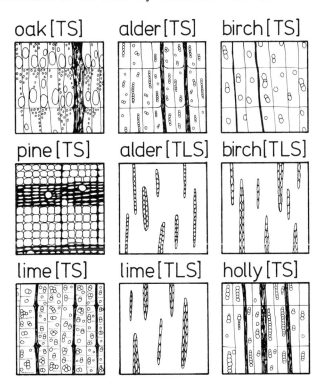

Fig. 14. Simplified microscopic structure of various woods in two of the identification sections shown in Fig. 13.

5
Identification of archaeological wood and charcoal

In order to identify individual species of wood some knowledge of the structure of wood is needed (fig. 13). To identify the species of wood it is necessary to cut a small cube from it showing three specific planes or to find on the object a clean section in each plane. The different planes show different patterns and these patterns vary from species to species (fig. 14). Some woods are easily identified with a hand lens (for example oak); others may be more difficult to identify unless a thin section can be cut and examined under a microscope. Waterlogged wood can be very soft so that it may be difficult to cut a clean facet to examine. Wood from buildings may be very hard and difficult to cut.

Many of the features that are used to identify archaeological wood are also present in charcoal. The great problem in the identification of charcoal is to get a clean face in all three sections and to light the surface adequately. Charcoals cannot be thin-sectioned and they tend to absorb light. The best sections for examination can be got by breaking the charcoal, sometimes with the help of a razor blade. The problem of light is best solved by using a microscope with through-the-lens lighting. Where this is not possible and if the charcoal is being examined at a lower magnification, adjustable high-wattage lights can be positioned to shine across the sections. The pieces of charcoal, when broken into the required planes, can be mounted in Plasticine to hold them steady while they are examined. The wood and charcoal sections can be examined and compared with photomicrographs but the ideal comparison is with sections of woods of known species. The accumulation of a reference collection is a high priority for anyone wishing to specialise in the identification of wood and charcoal.

Archaeological wood is a new and growing object of study and the preceding paragraphs only deal with the subject at a very superficial level. I hope that this introduction encourages the reader to follow up some of the further reading suggested in the bibliography. It is important to remember that many of the aspects of the study of archaeological wood, such as conservation and dendrochronology, are specialised subjects in their own right. However, anyone working in archaeology may be able to contribute to the growth of the subject because it is through an awareness of the possibilities of replaced wood, wood in locally wet environments and so on that new discoveries will be made.

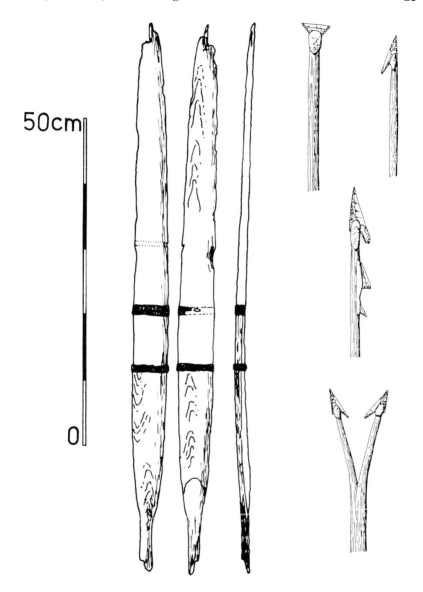

Fig. 15. *(Left)* The neolithic yew bow from Meare. *(Right)* Some tentative suggestions for the hafting of neolithic projectile points excavated at Fengate, Peterborough. (Drawing: F. M. M. Pryor.)

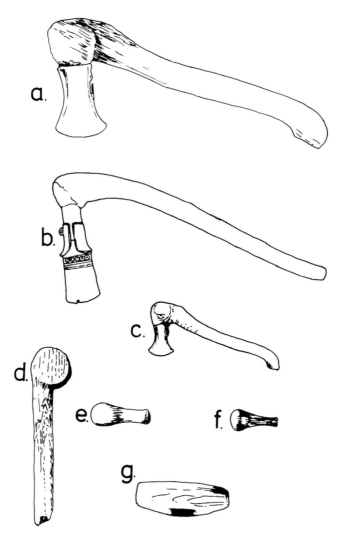

Fig. 16. (a) A bronze-age axe and handle from the river Boyne in Ireland. **(b)** A bronze-age axe and handle from Hallein, Austria. This handle was not preserved through waterlogging, as is usually the case, but survived instead in a salt mine, where it was abandoned. Salt is so toxic that insects, bacteria and fungi, which would normally attack the wood, were kept at bay. **(c)** Late bronze-age axe from the river Boyne at Edenberry. (After Evans.) **(d-g)** Iron-age wooden handles from the excavations at Glastonbury. **(d)** Handle of an unknown tool. **(e, f)** Small handles for awls or similar tools. **(g)** The T-handle of a spade or similar implement.

6
Types of wooden objects from archaeological sites

Arrowshafts (fig. 15)

A few arrowshafts have survived from the prehistoric period, sometimes in association with the resin that was used to secure the head to the shaft. Most prehistoric British arrowheads that have been found have been dated to the neolithic and there does not appear to have been much attempt at selecting particular woods for the purpose. Four arrows from one location in Somerset were all made of hazel but as hazel is one of the dominant species of shrub in the area it seems reasonable to assume that this was the reason for the selection of the wood. Generally, a wide selection of woods have been used for arrowshafts.

Axe handles (fig. 16)

Ash, the wood most commonly used for the purpose in modern times, is virtually unknown in the handles of prehistoric axes, whether stone or bronze. Indeed, there does not seem to have been any wood which was used preferentially. This begs the question as to whether all the axes of the prehistoric period were in fact used as axes in the accepted sense or were used for a greater diversity of activities. If the axes were not used for hard chopping but as wedges and for the general trimming of wood, then the qualities required of the handles may not have been so exacting.

Basketry (fig. 17)

Examples of basketwork have been found dating from the neolithic period onwards. It may be presumed that basketry would have been quite important, providing containers of all shapes and sizes as well as frameworks for lining with clay or covering with leather. Pits are occasionally lined with wickerwork too or it may be used as a form of revetment to stabilise the sides of a shallow well or waterhole. The woods that are most commonly associated with basketwork are willow and hazel and these frequently occur in the archaeological record, although other woods have occurred too. Any whippy young wood could be used for weaving and the types used may have depended upon what was required of the finished items.

Boats (fig. 18)

A very specialised branch of archaeological wood is the study of ancient wooden boats. Ancient wrecks have been found dating far back into prehistory, and dug-out boats are occasionally found buried in the muds and silts of riverbanks or old river courses. The study of

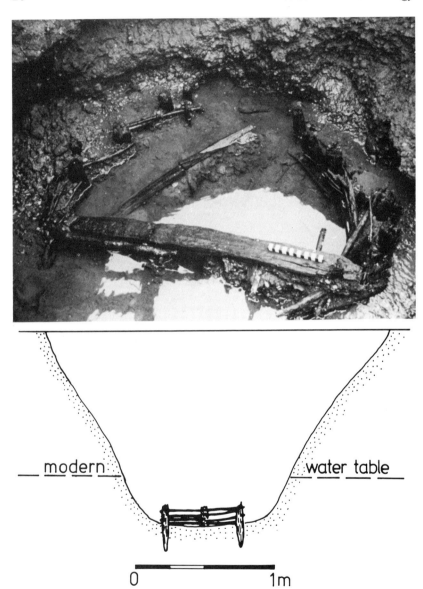

Fig. 17. Wicker must have been widely used in the past but is rarely preserved. Wicker was commonly used for lining storage pits. Here at Fengate, Peterborough, on a gravel soil with a high ground water table, the lining revetted the soft sides of this shallow well. (Photograph: F. M. M. Pryor.)

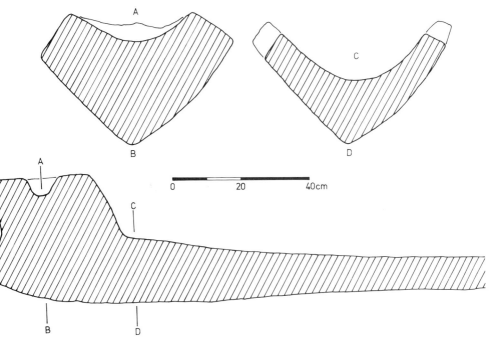

Fig. 18. Dug-out canoes or logboats have been widely studied and many may date from the bronze age. This example was found recently in Cambridgeshire, during maintenance of a fen drainage dyke; its date is uncertain, but most probably prehistoric because of the thickness of peat that had accumulated above it. (Drawing: E. Curry and the Nene Valley Research Committee.)

these boats and their conservation requires the resources of many specialists, from divers to nautical architects. The earliest evidence for boats comes from the mesolithic period. As the people of the time lived by hunting and gathering, especially along river valleys which formed after the last ice age, we may assume that they would have experimented with water transport. Most of the early boats which have been found – and there is a great increase in numbers in the bronze age – were made of oak. The study of these ancient boats also provides insight into the sophisticated woodworking techniques that were known to ancient man. There are very few other objects of wood that are likely to survive intact and in such numbers.

Bows (fig. 15)

Unlike arrowshafts, bows are remarkable for the selectivity shown in the woods used. Bows first appear in the neolithic period and they are invariably made of yew. Occasionally bows have occurred that are made of other woods, notably a bronze-age one made of oak, but

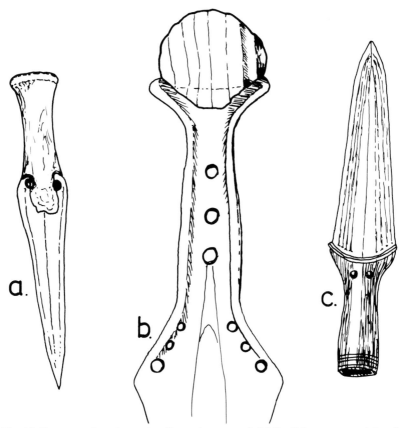

Fig. 19. Some sword or dagger handles and a pommel. **(a)** Small bronze-age oak-handled dagger from County Londonderry. **(b)** Wooden pommel of late bronze-age sword from Ballykillen, Ireland. **(c)** Yew handle of dagger from Arreton Down.

this is exceptional. Some bows were finely decorated and bound, but retrieving this sort of detail calls for very careful examination and conservation. The first bows for which we have evidence, those which were current more than four thousand years ago, look remarkably like the classic longbow of medieval times.

Boxes (fig. 1)

Boxes have appeared in the archaeological record and they would have provided simple and useful containers. Some of the standard joints were known from very early times and dowels were used extensively. Boxes, like other wooden containers, were probably widely used from earliest times but are not frequently preserved.

Clubs and mallets

A few objects which have been interpreted as clubs or mallets have been found and these have always been hard woods, not surprisingly. Oak and yew are the two common woods but there are good examples made of beech and holly.

Coffins

A number of early coffins have been found over the years, usually made out of hollowed tree trunks. These often date from the bronze age, but many of them were found in the nineteenth century and no attempt was made to identify the type of wood in many cases. Of those that have been identified, however, oak is the most common species.

Dagger and sword handles and pommels (fig. 19)

These handles are really grips rather than true handles and a variety of woods was used at all periods. Probably the availability of a wood was the most important factor together with the quality of the individual piece selected. Ash seems to have been used quite frequently, possibly because of its well known shock-absorbing qualities.

Looms (fig. 20)

Many looms may have been made in early times by driving posts into the ground as the basis for a frame. Parts of early looms were found in the lake village at Glastonbury. There is plenty of evidence from the Roman period and later for sophisticated looms.

Paddles

A number of wooden objects have been found over the years that have been described as paddles but it is possible that they are not all boat paddles. There is, for instance, one 'paddle' dated to the mesolithic which is made of birch wood, but birch is notoriously quick to rot in water and one wonders how long it would have lasted in use as a boat paddle. Also, although there are a considerable number of bronze-age boats, there do not appear to be any positively identified bronze-age paddles. This suggests that the boats were propelled by some other means, a pole for instance, or that there has been a remarkable accident of preservation.

Pins and points

A few pins and points have been found, made of various woods. These, not being tools for specific jobs, could probably have been made out of any wood that came to hand unless they needed to possess specific properties for a particular purpose.

Planks and boards

Planks and boards are not frequently found on archaeological excavations, presumably because such objects would not be thrown

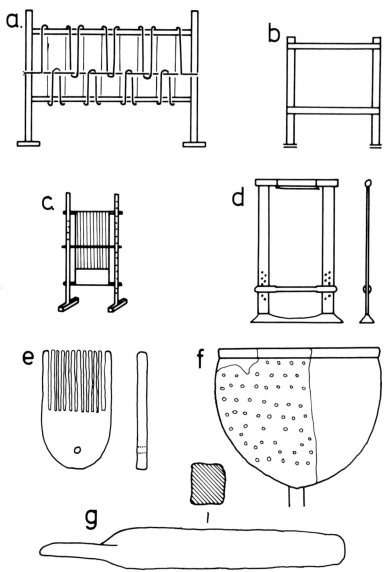

Fig. 20. Examples of weaving looms and other tools. **(a)** Iron-age two-beam loom from Den mark. **(b)** Two-beam loom from Rome. **(c)** Two-beam loom, as illustrated in a medieval manuscript. **(d)** Reconstruction of a loom from the Oseberg ship (scale 1:22). **(e)** Wooden ripping comb (scale 1:3). **(f)** Neolithic hackle (scale 1:3). **(g)** Neolithic scutching blade from Switzerland (scale 1:6). (After Wild.)

away while they still had a useful life. Some have been found in the Somerset Levels as part of the construction of neolithic and bronze-age trackways across the peat (fig. 21). A number of planks have also been found associated with burials, a plank being used rather like a coffin in some burials during the bronze age. Most of these pieces of wood that have been identified seem to be oak, with one or two pieces of elm and ash, all of which are good timber species. Before effective saws became available planks and boards would have been made by splitting the wood. Wood is likely to split in a number of ways and the skill of the craftsman lay in using the natural tendency of the wood to best advantage (fig. 22).

Platforms

Platforms are usually structures laid down at the edge of water to make a solid surface for people to move about on. Several are known from the mesolithic period, which was a time when people were closely associated with water and often chose to live near it. These platforms were often made of brushwood, which probably represented what was available locally. Platforms from the mesolithic, neolithic and bronze age all appear to have been made out of woods such as pine, birch and alder.

Posts, poles and stakes

Archaeologists are used to finding evidence for posts, poles and stakes in the form of the post and stake holes left in the ground, but when the conditions are right the wood itself may be preserved. The bronze-age waterfront at Runnymede has recently been uncovered and excavated. The riverbank here was revetted with large posts, generally of oak, which were in an excellent state of preservation when they were uncovered (fig. 23).

Sheaths and scabbards

Sheaths and scabbards for swords and daggers have occurred occasionally and there is one find of a sheath for a bronze-age razor. Chapes have often been found; these are the metal tips, often decorated, of scabbards, but as the scabbards themselves are usually made of organic material they survive less frequently. They seem often to have been made of thin laths of wood with leather coverings, inside and out. A fragment from Pyotdykes in Scotland shows one way in which they were constructed. This fragment consists of a thin lath of hazel inserted between the layers of one skin which has been split. This fragment was preserved adhering to the sword. Other swords and daggers have been noted as having wood or leather in association but few have been studied as thoroughly as this piece. There is not much evidence for the types of wood used in the construction of scabbards although most of the identified bronze-age ones are of hazel. In the iron age a greater variety of woods seems to have been used, including ash, birch and yew.

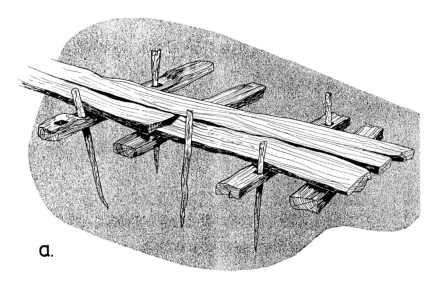

a.

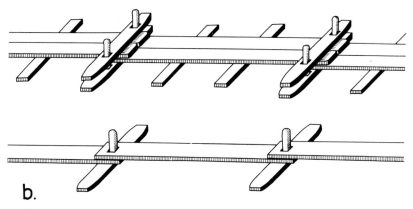

b.

Fig. 21. Reconstruction drawings of two ancient trackways based on recent excavations. **(a)** The Meare Heath trackway, Somerset Levels. (Drawing: J. M. Coles.) **(b)** A remarkably similar construction, also prehistoric, from Holland. (Drawing: Casparie and van Zeist.)

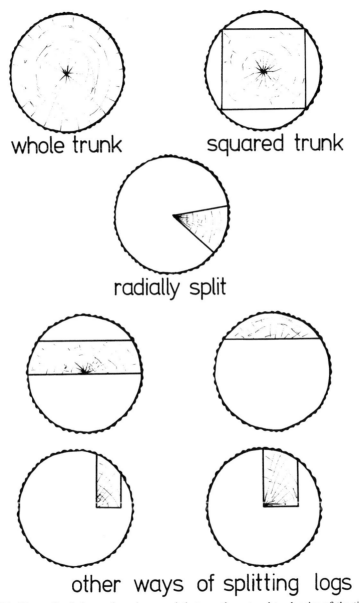

whole trunk squared trunk

radially split

other ways of splitting logs

Fig. 22. Ways of splitting and sawing wood that use the natural tendencies of the timber.

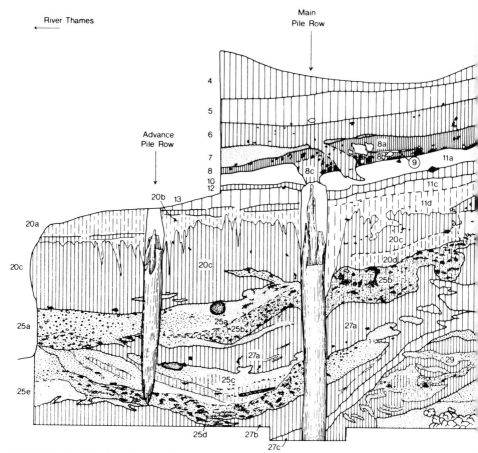

River Thames

Main
Pile Row

Advance
Pile Row

Fig. 23. Section drawing showing the archaeological deposits of the bronze-age waterfront site recently excavated at Runnymede Bridge, Surrey. This drawing illustrates the complexity of such sites; the large wooden piles which formed the river front can be seen to the left of the section. (Drawing: S. Needham.)

Shields

There have been a few shields and shield bases from archaeological contexts, mostly bronze-age in date. All the identified examples are of alder, which is a soft wood and easily worked. Leather shields made by building up leather on to wooden moulds have been proved by experiment to have offered good protection.

Spearshafts (fig. 24)

There are strong possibilities for the preservation of wood in association with spearheads from the bronze age and iron age. They

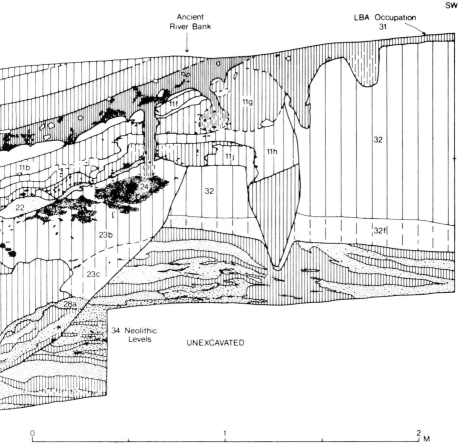

would all originally have had wooden shafts attached to them, and, especially where the shaft had to be pushed far up into a socket, the wood may well have been preserved. A large number of spearheads, especially those dating from the bronze age, have produced wood fragments which are the remains of the shafts, and new ones are being discovered as more people examine their finds with care. There appears to have been a strong element of selection in the types of wood used for these hafts. By far the most common wood found in this context is ash and at present ash wood probably accounts for about half of all the bronze-age spearshafts known. Ash is still the main wood used for the handles of agricultural and horticultural implements.

Structures

Generally the evidence for wood from houses and similar structures comes in the form of wood remains from posts and beams or carbonised remains if the structure has been burnt down. Most large

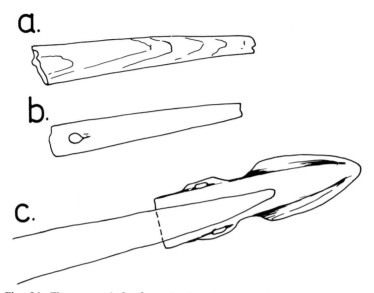

Fig. 24. Three spearshafts from the late bronze-age hoard at Wilburton near Ely, Cambridgeshire. One is carbonised, but the others probably owe their preservation to their close proximity to bronze. The copper in bronze is highly toxic and wood in close contact with it would be protected from insect, bacterial or fungal attack.

structures, including mortuary houses from under barrows, seem to have been made almost exclusively of oak, which would have been eminently suitable as it is strong and resilient. Oak has been widely used as a structural timber throughout history and prehistory. The great timbers of the medieval waterfront at Hull were all of oak (fig. 25).

Swords

Wooden swords would have had only limited capabilities but may have been used as replicas of metal originals, although a wooden sword made of yew, of which there is a bronze-age example, would have been fairly tough.

Tools (fig. 26)

Forks have been found along with other agricultural tools. Several ards have been found, mostly in bogs, and experiments have shown that wooden ards can cut the soil quite efficiently.

Tracks (fig. 21)

Corduroy roads and tracks over wet ground made out of wood have occurred in several parts of Britain and Europe. They were constructed from the neolithic period onwards and generally used a great variety of woods, which were presumably found close by. The most intensively studied wooden trackways are in Somerset. Tracks were constructed in a number of ways, from throwing down bundles of brushwood to carefully constructed railway-like structures and basketwork hurdles fastened down into the soft earth beneath (fig. 27).

Troughs and vessels (fig. 28)

Wooden vessels of various kinds have been discovered, dating from all periods from the neolithic onwards. Wooden vessels would have

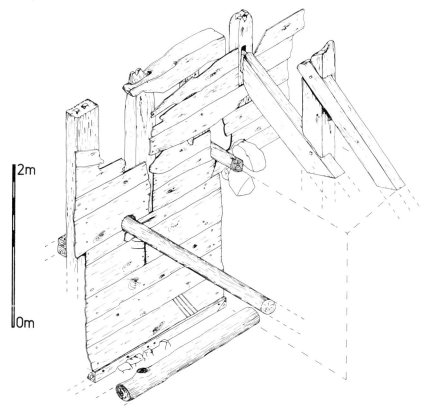

Fig. 25. Medieval waterfront recently excavated in Hull by the East Riding Archaeological Society. The massive timbers are of oak. (Isometric drawing by C. K. Brown.)

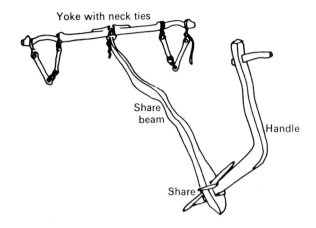

Yoke with neck ties

Share
beam

Handle

Share

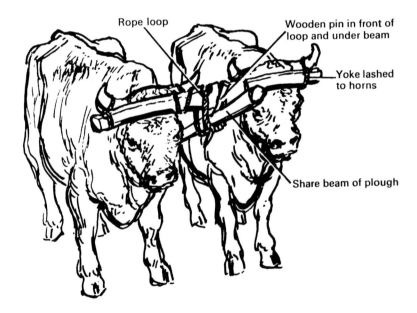

Rope loop

Wooden pin in front of
loop and under beam

Yoke lashed
to horns

Share beam of plough

Fig. 26. Reconstruction of an iron-age ard (plough), based on remains from a peat bog in Denmark. The ard simply cut a furrow in the soil, unlike the plough, which turns the soil over. (Illustrations by Valerie Bell from *Farming in the Iron Age* by Peter J. Reynolds, Cambridge University Press.)

Fig. 27. The Walton Heath track, in the Somerset Levels, dated by radiocarbon to about 2300 BC. Most of the panels in the central area are damaged but all are in their original positions. Long poles lie beside the panels on both sides and the central part of this area is raised by the four levels of wood placed under it. Scale totals one metre. (Photograph: J. M. Coles.)

been useful pieces of equipment, especially as they would have been less fragile than pottery, and serviceable platters and such like could have been made quite easily. Identified examples seem often to have been made of oak, with ash and alder occurring occasionally.

Twigs and branches

Twigs and branches may occur on any site where there are waterlogged deposits. Usually these represent litter and rubbish that have fallen into wet holes or ponds. Little can be deduced from the examination of this sort of material because usually nothing is known of how it would have found its way into the archaeological deposit. It is not always possible to assume that the twigs and so on represent species growing nearby, as they may be only the trimmings from larger pieces of wood that had been brought to the site for a specific purpose, and possibly from some distance away. When twiggy material is first uncovered on a site, however, it may not be immediately apparent whether it is simply a mass of small pieces of wood or part of something larger, such as a wicker lining to a pit or a brush drain (fig. 29).

Wheels

There is evidence for both spoked and disc wheels by the iron age. Disc wheels have been found in the Irish bogs. These are usually made of three planks held together with dowels. One of these wheels was made of alder, which is a very soft wood, but perhaps it was a useful wood for a wheel that was built to run over wet ground because it is so resistant to decay. At Glastonbury a turned axle box and wheel spoke have been found and a beautifully preserved iron-age wheel was found at Holme Pierrepoint (fig. 30).

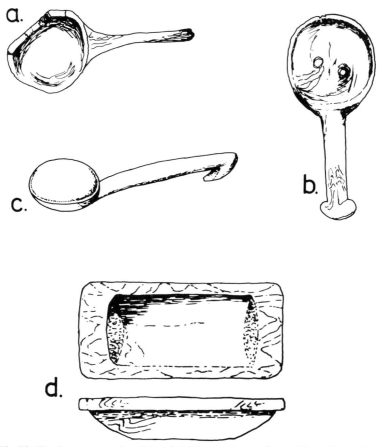

Fig. 28. Wooden spoons and a platter. **(a, b)** Spoons (one perforated) from Glastonbury iron-age settlement. **(c)** Modern wooden spoon made in a traditional fashion. **(d)** Platter from Glastonbury of a type that was probably very common in the iron age but which rarely survives.

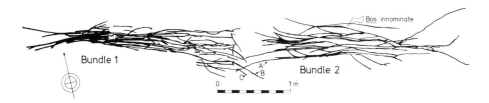

Fig. 29. Late iron-age willow brush drain laid along the bottom of a ditch on the fen edge at Fengate, Peterborough. The surviving part of the drain consists of two bundles of osiers laid end to end at the same time (note that twigs A, B and C intertwine); the wood was cut from coppiced or pollarded trees after seven or eight years of growth. This example illustrates the importance of exposing sufficiently large areas of waterlogged wood, for what at first may seem to be a mass of twigs may turn out to have both form and an apparent function. (Photograph: F. M. M. Pryor.)

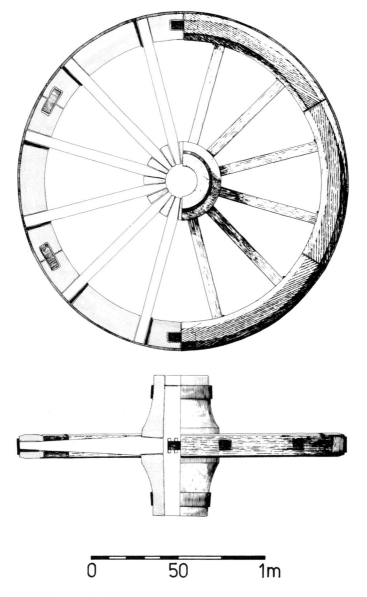

Fig. 30. A fine iron-age wheel from Holme Pierrepoint in the Trent valley, Nottinghamshire. It has since been conserved and represents a sophisticated piece of woodworking technology. (Drawing: I. Stead.)

7

Types of wood and their uses

Alder *Alnus glutinosa* also known as black or European alder

Alder is a well known tree of the wetlands. It grows abundantly in fen woods, requiring a base-rich soil with a high moisture content. The wood of alder is not regarded very highly as a fuel, although it burns well if seasoned. The charcoal is excellent and is used in gun-powder. The bark of the alder has been used in tanning in the past. Several dyes can be obtained from different parts of the tree. The bark produces a red dye; a pinky-fawn colour comes from the fresh wood, green from the catkins and yellow from the young shoots. The timber is soft and when dry it is weak and perishable. But the softness of the timber makes it easier to work and it does not split easily. It has often been used, therefore, for turning, for wooden shoes and for carving. A useful characteristic of this timber is that it is extremely durable under water. It has been widely used for revetting riverbanks, boatbuilding and pumps. One specific use of the wood is in the glassmaking in-dustry. Alder-wood blocks are widely favoured for glass moulds. The wood produces such a soft carbon layer that very little wood-grain pattern is transferred to the hot glass. Alder wood has been found regularly in various tracks in the Somerset Levels, but especially on the Abbot's Way track. An ard beam from Lochmaben was alder wood. This ard was dated to *c* 80 BC. A wooden tub of alder contain-ing a late bronze-age hoard of bronze was found in the Fens (fig. 31).

Apple *Malus sylvestris* also known as crab or wild apple, wilding

Wild apples are ubiquitous in their distribution. The fruit is usually unpalatable unless treated in some way such as fermentation or in a jelly. Apple wood burns well and gives off a pleasant smell. Apple-wood shavings give a distinctive flavour if used for smoking fish and have been used for this purpose in East Anglia. The timber from apple is usually only available in small pieces. It is hard but easy to work and is often used for carving. Crab apples have often survived in prehistoric storage pits and it is generally thought that they were dried and stored for winter food. Apples are also represented in the archaeological record by the presence of pip impressions on prehistoric pottery: pip impressions survive on six separate potsherds at the neolithic site of Windmill Hill.

Ash *Fraxinus excelsior* also known as European ash

Ash is a native tree on base-rich, damp soils in Britain, although it does appear less commonly on sandy soils. It is sensitive to heavy frosts. Ash is a fine fuel, burning well, even when green. Ash-wood shavings have been used for smoking kippers in East Anglia. It is also an important timber because it is strong and resilient with a very close straight grain, although it rots easily in contact with the ground. It is remarkable for its elasticity, which is why it is so widely used for handles, hafts and shafts, for oars and for barrel hoops. It is an important timber for general carpentry and is probably the most important source of timber after oak and beech. As might be expected, a useful wood such as ash has appeared in archaeological contexts. The cross-battens in the Ferriby boat were of ash (middle bronze age) and there are examples of arrowshafts made of ash.

Beech *Fagus sylvatica* also known as European beech

Beech trees occur commonly on chalky soils and are often associated with the chalk lands. They also appear on well drained sands, however, as their limiting factor is the drainage and they cannot survive on waterlogged soils. They are tolerant of base-poor soils and will also grow in the shade, under oak trees for instance. At present they are limited in their distribution in Britain to the south because they are affected by low summer temperatures and late frosts. The nuts are edible but they are small and are not abundant every year. There is evidence for the extraction of oil from the nuts. There was a large industry based on the extraction of beech-nut oil in Germany during the two world wars. This oil is edible and non-drying and has been used for soap production and for lighting. It is used as a cooking oil in France and can be made into margarine. The wood is an excellent fuel, burning with little smoke but a good deal of heat. Distillation of the wood yields tar, creosote and methyl alcohol, and the leaves have been used to stuff mattresses as they are slightly toxic and so discourage infestation by pests. The wood is valuable. It is hard and durable with an even grain. Its strength depends on the seasoning, as it is prone to warp and crack if it is not well seasoned. It can be difficult to work when dry but it is generally considered to be an extremely useful and attractive timber. It has been used extensively for turning and carving as well as for furniture. It is durable under water and has been used in shipbuilding as well as for small dams. Beech wood has been used in the Somerset Levels trackways, as well as for stone axe handles and spearshafts.

Birch *Betula pendula* also known as silver birch, white birch; *Betula pubescans* also known as downy birch, white birch

The silver birch is abundant on heaths and gravels, shallow peats and light soils and it can survive at high altitudes. It cannot, however, tolerate shade, growing only in the open or in clearings. *Betula pubescans* is more common on damper heath soils. The only reported use of birch as a food is in the preparation of wine from the sap. The wood is much used as a fuel. The charcoal is also excellent and was

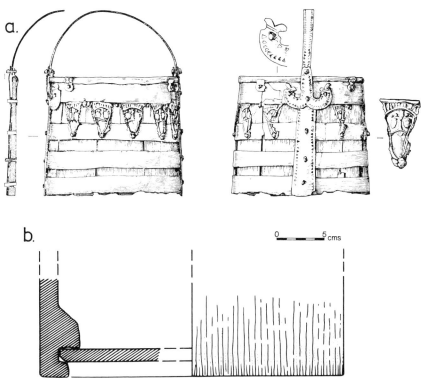

Fig. 31. Examples of wooden containers. **(a)** Stave-built Saxon bucket from recent excavations at Mucking, Essex. (Drawing: Judith Dobie, Ancient Monuments Drawing Office. Crown Copyright.) **(b)** Wooden tub from Stuntney Fen, Cambridgeshire. It contained a hoard of bronze-age metal tools and weapons. It is of a type that is commonly found but rarely dated and is made from a hollowed alder log with the base fitted into an internal groove around the bottom.

widely used for iron smelting in the past. A by-product of the wood as fuel is the smoke, which is often used in Scotland for smoking herrings. Over the centuries the trees have been widely exploited for a variety of commodities. The bark has an important property in that it can be sewn. It can be detached from the tree in thin strips and is easily worked. There are many good examples of birch-bark containers from Europe. The bark has also been used for tanning and as an insulation. As it is impervious it has been used locally in Europe and Asia for roofing shingles. The bark also contains a high proportion of pitch so that rolled pieces burn with a clear flame. If this pitch is extracted and prepared it can make a useful glue. There is some evidence that the tree has also been a source of bast fibre. Birch timber rots quickly in water, and so it has been used extensively for furniture, doors, plywood and so on rather than for external work. In Britain it rarely grows large or straight enough to produce useful timber. Birch figures extensively in the archaeological record. There are the birch-bark containers, and the wood has been used for arrowshafts. This use is not surprising as the wood is tough and elastic. It is commercially classed as perishable but if it is seasoned properly it is as strong as oak as well as being easily worked.

Box *Buxus sempervirens*
    Box is native on chalk and limestone in Britain. The wood is hard and not easily split but it can be planed and turned. It is very close-grained and dense, properties that have led to its use for printing blocks, small wheels, pins, screws, shuttles, buttons, rulers and musical instruments. Although the wood is so hard, dense and heavy, it is technically a softwood and is a good illustration of the fact that the words 'hard' and 'soft' applied to wood are names and not descriptions. The other use of the trees is as ornamental plants or in hedges. Exploitation of the timber was probably limited because it was not available in large pieces. The wood has occurred archaeologically from time to time. A Roman boxwood comb was found in Wales and box was extensively used in Europe for lining coffins, which may account for its common name. Box hedge clippings from the Roman site at Winterton also attest the use of the plant for hedging from an early date.

Cherry *Prunus padus* also known as bird cherry; *Prunus avium* also known as wild cherry, gean, mazzard; *Prunus cerasus* also known as sour cherry, dwarf cherry; *Prunus spinosa* also known as sloe, blackthorn
    All these plants like a base-rich soil and thrive on heavy or damp ground. They do not respond well to coppicing or pollarding and seem to prefer open ground rather than woodland. The different types of *Prunus* vary in their requirements but only to a limited extent. The fruits are also used for different purposes. The gean fruit can be eaten raw. The sour cherry, as might be expected from its name, is less palatable but it is used commercially for flavouring liqueurs, and the seed or 'stone' can be used to produce a semi-drying oil (cherry kernel oil). This may be refined for use as a salad oil or in the production of cosmetics. The bird cherry is also used as a flavouring for brandy and wines, and the fruit can be made into a preserve. The sloe produces a very acid berry, which is inedible raw although it can be made into jellies and sloe gin. The wood is a difficult fuel to ignite but once it is alight it burns very well. The wood varies among the species of *Prunus* but it is all hard and fine-grained and is prized for cabinet making. It was used for walking sticks, particularly Irish shillelaghs. Archaeologically, cherry 'stones' are quite common. A wheelbarrow full of sloe stones was recovered from the Glastonbury lake village. It is possible that the fruit was used for producing dye.

Elder *Sambucus nigra* also known as European elder
The berries and flowers are both edible, although they are usually consumed in the form of wine. Elder can reproduce by seed and is also suitable for coppicing. It has been a useful source of raw materials in the past. The wood has been used for cogs in mills when hornbeam was unavailable. It has also been used for pegs and butcher's skewers. Elder bark is a source of black dye and the pith from the stem can be used to hold specimens for cutting to make microscope slides. That elder may have been a useful plant in the prehistoric period is indicated by finds of elderberries in prehistoric storage pits.

Elm *Ulmus glabra, Ulmus campestre* also known as wych elm, Scots elm; *Ulmus procera* also known as English elm
Wych elm is abundant in north and west Britain and is often to be seen pollarded. English elm has similar properties but it tends to sucker rather than to grow from seed so that it was often found in hedges before Dutch elm disease caused so much destruction. Today there are many hybrid elms with varying habits and characteristics. Elm leaves have been much used for animal fodder until recent times. The new tissue in the wych elm tree can be made into 'bark bread', which is a good source of bulk food for humans. The wood from the elm is tough, hard and very resistant to splitting. It is also resistant to rotting as long as it remains either wet or dry and is not allowed to change from one extreme to the other. It is used for butcher's blocks and the felloes of wheels because it does not split easily. Because of its resistance to decay it was used in shipbuilding, drains and coffins. The main revetments in the waterfront at Trig Lane in London were made with elm for the piles. Elm has also been widely used for bridge building in lowland Britain since earliest medieval times.

Guelder rose *Viburnum opulus*
The guelder rose is a shrub of damp places, in bogs and beside streams. The red fruits of the shrub are inedible raw because they contain valerianic acid. They are occasionally eaten cooked, however, and made into jellies. The wood has been used in modern times for butcher's skewers and has also appeared in the archaeological record in a late bronze-age trackway in Somerset (Shapwick Heath). Neolithic arrowshafts made from this wood have been found in Scotland and Denmark.

Hawthorn *Crataegus monogyna* also known as whitethorn, quickthorn, may; *Crataegus oxycanthoides* also known as English hawthorn, midland hawthorn, woodland hawthorn
Quickthorn is a common hedge plant and also occurs in scrub. It is generally a characteristic plant of open habitats. English hawthorn is a shade-tolerant woodland species. It is impossible to separate the species by their wood. The leaves of the quickthorn are edible and

there is some evidence from mainland Europe that the haws have been collected for food. The wood is hard, heavy and difficult to work. It is, however, fine-grained and has been used for turning, wagon parts and for walking sticks.

Hazel *Corylus avellana* also known as cobnut, nuttery, European hazel

The hazel can tolerate a wide variety of soils and is abundant on chalk and limestone as well as neutral and mildly alkaline soils. It is also recorded at altitudes as high as 2,000 feet (600 metres). The hazel is a well known source of food. The nuts, known variously as Barcelona nuts, cobnuts, filberts or hazel nuts, are not only tasty but also highly nutritious. They can be crushed to produce an oil, which has been used for food, lubricants, soaps, perfumes and paints. The leaves can be eaten by human beings and sheep but cattle do not like them. The wood makes a reasonable fuel and a regular supply can easily be ensured because of the tree's success when coppiced. Left to grow freely, the hazel can become a medium-sized tree. It is rarely seen as such, however, because when it is coppiced it produces large amounts of useful wood. Trees coppiced every seven years produce poles of suitable size for making sheep hurdles. Thinner hazel wood is used by thatchers for spars. Generally, the young flexible wood can be used for all kinds of hurdling, fencing and basketry. The wood is of little use when older, being soft and light. It has occasionally been used for such items as walking sticks and light aircraft. Archaeological evidence for hazel appears quite frequently. It has been used extensively in the construction of tracks in the Somerset Levels as well as for arrowshafts, a spear and a bow. A late bronze-age sword scabbard from Scotland was made of leather stiffened with a lath of hazel. There are also many examples of wicker-lined pits.

Holly *Ilex aquifolium* also known as English holly, hulver

Holly is native to the British Isles except for the far north as it cannot stand hard frosts. It is often found under beech and oak wood, in hedges in some areas and on rocky hillsides. It is very tolerant of poor soils. Holly wood is a fast burning fuel. Logs of holly will burn with a bright flame but do not give out a great deal of heat. The wood is hard and fine-grained and so has been widely used for carving and turning, for handles, inlay and veneer. Some of the pegs used in the construction of the Sweet Track were made of holly and a 'hooked implement' has also been found there.

Hornbeam *Carpinus betulus* also known as European hornbeam, hardbeam

The hornbeam is native to south-east England but is susceptible to spring frosts. It is not well adapted to coastal regions and this limits its distribution. Hornbeam is a valuable fuel both as wood and as charcoal. In the past trees have been lopped for firewood and extensive coppices existed on the North Downs and at Epping for the supply of wood and charcoal. The tree regularly appears in hedges and is well adapted to coppicing and pollarding, although it does not produce suckers. The trees are not large and the wood is very tough and hard with a great resistance to shearing. Because of these properties it has been extensively used for mallet heads, axles, spokes, yokes, cogs and handles. The archaeological occurrence of the wood bears out the modern use although worked hornbeam is only occasionally found. A wagon from a bog in Denmark is an example where hornbeam wood was used for the spokes of the wheels.

Juniper *Juniperus communis*

The juniper is native on the chalk lands in the south of Britain and on the limestone in the north. It used to grow on the Scottish moors in some quantity and is resistant to grazing. As it is not resistant to fire, however, it has been greatly reduced by the burning of the heather. It is best suited to cool, wet conditions. Juniper berries have been used as a flavouring for a number of dishes, although their best known and most appreciated use is for flavouring gin. In Norway the berries are used for flavouring beer. They are also a source of oil. Juniper foliage is sometimes used for kindling. The bark of the juniper has been used as a source of cordage in Lapland; the roots have been made into baskets and a brown dye has been made from the berries. The wood does not rank highly as a timber, although it has occasionally been used for the handles of daggers and spoons.

Larch *Larix decidua* also known as European larch

It is thought that the larch was introduced in the seventeenth century. The timber from the larch is very durable and has been much used for posts and poles. The wood is also a source of turpentine, whilst the bark is rich in tannin.

Lime *Tilia cordata* also known as small-leaved lime; *Tilia platyphyllos* also known as large-leaved lime

Both kinds of lime prefer base-rich soils. The small-leaved lime occurs as a native throughout England and Wales, but especially on limestone. The large-leaved lime may be an early introduction to Britain, but it occurs freely from early times on limestone soils in the Wye valley and in South Yorkshire. The two species hybridise readily, so that pure strains are rare. Most modern limes are hybrids but they are all good for pollarding and coppicing. Limes are probably the most thermophilous (warmth-loving species) in Britain and are generally used as an indicator of deteriorating climate. Young lime leaves are edible; they are certainly well browsed by animals, especially deer. An indirect source of food comes from the flowers, which bees love and which produce good honey. Bast fibres from lime are very fine and much sought after. Unfortunately the gathering of bast is destructive to the tree. The wood is light and fine, strong and attractive. It splits quite easily and has considerable longitudinal strength. The wood has been favoured by carvers; Grinling Gibbons used it extensively. Bast fibres from lime must have been very important in ancient times. They were widely used in medieval times for halters, tope and fishing tackle.

Maple *Acer campestre* also known as field maple, hedge maple; *Acer pseudoplatanus* also known as sycamore, plane, Scotch or great maple

The field maple is a native tree in Britain and is common on calcareous soils. It occurs in England and Wales from southern Cumbria and Durham southwards, although it appears to be resistant of frost in England. It can tolerate shade and therefore may grow into a substantial woodland tree, although it is found more frequently today as an undershrub or hedge plant. There is very little to suggest that the tree has ever been important as a source of food although sap bled from the trunk has been used in making ale. Similarly the wood does not seem to figure much as a fuel. The wood is light brown, light in weight and texture, even when wet, and tough. Because of its smooth texture it has been widely used for textile and laundry rollers. It turns well and has been used for bowls and inlay. The wood of the field maple is rarely available today. Field maple wood has been found in the Somerset Levels and a prehistoric yoke found on the European mainland was made of maple wood. The sycamore is a late introduction and not generally important for archaeologists.

Mountain ash *Sorbus aucuparia* also known as European mountain ash, rowan, quicken; *Sorbus aria* also known as whitebeam

Both trees are native to Britain. The rowan is abundant in the northern half of the country and at high altitudes. The whitebeam tends to grow more in chalk and limestone country. The rowan is very tolerant of poor soils and can be usefully coppiced. The berries are rich in vitamin C and have been used for flavouring jellies and for flavouring brandy in Germany and vodka in Russia. The leaves and flowers have been used for herbal tea and also for adulterating tea. The wood is very fine and close-grained and is useful because it is also hard, tough and elastic. Its use has been limited because it is usually only available in small pieces. It occurs quite frequently, therefore, as tool handles and as small parts, often turned, in spinning wheels and wagons.

Oak *Quercus petraea* also known as sessile oak, durmast; *Quercus robur* also known as English oak, pedunculate oak

The sessile oak is the dominant tree in the north and west of Britain and is found mixed with the pedunculate oak on light soils in the south. It occurs at altitudes of up to 1700 feet (450 metres) on Dartmoor. Both species can be successfully coppiced or pollarded and both appear to be quite tolerant of poor soils. Acorns are very bitter but they are edible roasted. The acorn is valued as animal fodder, especially for pigs. Oak is an excellent fuel, both as wood and charcoal. It was oak charcoal that was used in the iron-smelting industry in Sussex. In East Anglia oak shavings were used for smoking kippers, and oak billets for smoking bloaters. (Bloaters are smoked whole.) The whole of the oak tree is rich in tannic acid and the bark has been widely used in the tanning industry. Most of the tannin is in the inner, bast layers. Leaf galls are also a source of tannin. Oak wood is well known for its properties of strength, beauty and durability. It splits well (fig. 22) and has considerable longitudinal strength. The sapwood is more perishable and was generally avoided. Throughout history and prehistory oak was widely used for all kinds of carpentry, from fine furniture to ships, docks and lock gates. Archaeologically, oak is probably the most common wood found, whether as wood or charcoal. Oak trunks were used for everything from dug-out boats and coffins to waterfronts. Oak splits well longitudinally and was thus well suited for making planks, beams and for shaping into smaller objects.

Pear *Pyrus communis*
The pear is less able to stand extremes of temperature than the apple. It is not clear whether it is native to Britain, but it does appear in archaeological deposits from the neolithic onwards and may well have been cultivated from that time. Most of the evidence for the tree comes from the southern counties of England. The fruit of the wild pear is very acid when raw but can be cooked and made into jelly. The wood is highly prized as fuel, and the leaves can be used to produce a yellow dye. The wood is good for carving, for making rulers and drawing instruments. It is a heavy and durable wood, used for turnery and knife handles. The wood has also been used for the blocks of glass moulds, because it produces a fine carbon layer on contact with molten glass.

Pine *Pinus sylvestris* also known as Scots pine
The pine is tolerant of poor soils, hence its tendency to grow in association with acid peat. Pine trees are susceptible to clearance, as they can easily be burnt off, and, unlike trees that can be coppiced and pollarded, once felled they die. Pine wood burns hotly and rapidly; the reasons for this become obvious when the materials that can be obtained from the wood are examined. Pine-wood products can be distilled to produce pitch and tar, as well as turpentine. The leaves produce an oil and the cones are a source of yellow dye. Pine timber is not strong but it is very durable and has been used for planking and general carpentry. A bronze-age longbow from Ostergötland was made of pine, probably because the area was too cold to produce yew, which is the usually favoured wood. There have also been finds of arrowshafts made of pine. It was probably an important tree in areas where others would not thrive.

Poplar *Populus nigra* also known as black poplar; *Populus tremula* also known as aspen

The aspen, although native to Britain, is probably at the most northern extent of its range. The old native forms of the poplar have been squeezed out by imported hybrids in Britain. The black poplars are not woodland trees and tend to grow along stream sides. Aspens, however, are occasionally found along the edges of wet woodlands. Poplar wood is not a good fuel. Unless it is burned in small pieces and thoroughly dried first it is difficult to make it burn at all. The timber, too, is not highly prized. It is soft, coarse and light and has been used for such items as matchsticks, Camembert cheese boxes and Dutch clogs.

Sweet chestnut *Castanea sativa* also known as Spanish chestnut

The sweet chestnut is not a native of the British Isles; it may have been a Roman introduction. It is a very common tree on light soils and is known to be a warmth-loving species. The chestnuts are edible raw but are better roasted. They can also be boiled, made into flour, soup, fried in oil or used in confectionery. The Romans used chestnut flour and also fed the nuts to pigs. The wood is not a good fuel because it tends to smoulder and does not burn brightly. It is useful in other respects, however. It is very resistant to weathering and is widely used for paling fences, poles and similar outdoor work. The wood is more prone to splitting than oak, and this property is taken advantage of in the production of cleft palings. Chestnut is commercially classed as being as durable as oak, but it is not as hard or as tough. It is easy to work but difficult to season.

Willow *Salix alba* also known as white willow; *Salix viminalis* also known as osier; *Salix caprea* also known as sallow, goat willow; *Salix fragilis* also known as crack willow

There are in Britain a number of native willows, all of which have similar requirements for their healthy growth and development, and all of which are suitable for pollarding and coppicing. They are important as timber trees as well as being a source of other raw materials on the wetlands. Willow is the tree that is associated, more than any other, with water — and a vast amount of water is required to keep a willow healthy. An infusion made from willow bark has long been a folk remedy for headaches and rheumatism, which is not surprising as aspirin was first produced from this bark. Willow makes a reasonable fuel when it is well dried, burning with little smoke. The charcoal is of excellent quality. Willow must have been a very valuable tree in antiquity. The bark contains tannin, as well as aspirin, so the folk remedy referred to above must have been a powerful decoction. Deep red dyes can be prepared from the roots and strong fibres are obtainable from the bast. Willow wood is very resilient and therefore has been used for such items as cricket bats and artificial legs. The timber is fine and straight-grained. Many willows are still coppiced or pollarded for different kinds of wood: the young stems (withies or osiers) are used for baskets or wickerwork; poles are widely used for fencing and when cleft thinly have been made into hurdles, sieves and fruit baskets. The finest wood was often set aside for making milking pails. It may be difficult to separate willow from poplar in the identification of wood from archaeological deposits. The usefulness of the tree, especially in wet areas where other trees would not thrive, should not be underestimated.

Yew *Taxus baccata* also known as English yew
Yews are native on the chalkland in southern England and they require well drained land. Almost all parts of the yew are poisonous to both animals and humans. Yew is technically a softwood but it is very hard and dense. The wood is close-grained and flexible and so has long been the preferred species in the construction of bows. Because of its irregular growth pattern yew has also been favoured as a decorative wood, for turning and carving. The most famous piece of yew, archaeologically, must be the Clacton 'spear point', which has been dated to the Hoxnian Interglacial. Prehistoric bows in Europe are generally made of yew, just as their medieval counterparts were.

Bibliography

Clapham, A. R. et al. *Excursion Flora of the British Isles*. Cambridge University Press, 1968.

Coles, J. M. (ed). *The Somerset Levels Papers*. The Somerset Levels Project, Department of Archaeology, University of Cambridge, or Department of History, University of Exeter; annually since 1975.

Coles, J. M. and Orme, B. J. *The Prehistory of the Somerset Levels*. Somerset Levels Project, 1980.

Dimbleby, G. *Plants and Archaeology*. Paladin Books, 1978.

Edlin, H. L. *Woodland Crafts in Britain*. David and Charles, 1974.

Everett, T. H. *Living Trees of the World*. Thames and Hudson, 1969.

Jane, F. W. *The Structure of Wood*. Adam and Charles Black, 1956.

Mitchell, A. *A Field Guide to Trees of Britain and Northern Europe*. Collins, 1974.

Morgan, R. A. 'The selection and sampling of timber from archaeological sites for identification and tree ring analysis.' *The Journal of Archaeological Science*, 2, 221-30, 1975.

Pennington, W. *The History of the British Vegetation*. English Universities Press, second edition 1974.

Rackham, O. *Trees and Woodlands in the British Landscape*. Dent, 1976.

Western, C. 'Wood and charcoal in archaeology' in Brothwell, D. and Higgs, E. S. *Science in Archaeology* 188-90, 1969.

Index